The Bruises From My Mother's Love

By

Author Danette

Copyright

ABOUT THE BOOK

This is the story of Lunye' Williams, a woman who suffered horrific physical, mental and sexual abuse at the hands of her mother and other family members from the time she was a child until she became a teenager.

Read how Lunye' survived the blistering welts and the blood-filled bruises received from her mother from the age of five to thirteen years old.

Each book will let you in on how she endured and survived her abusive mother along with other adversaries and serve as inspiration for every reader as they cope with the struggles in their own lives.

Words to my Readers

Proverbs 6: 5

Free yourself like a gazelle from the hand of the hunter, like a bird from the snare of the fowler

Dedication

This novel is dedicated to the youth and the parents that can relate to situations of current and past abuse.

The burden that you carry may be heavy, but know that your suffering has not gone in vain. Let your pain and your torture be your stepping stone to your success.

As you may see in this series of my life.

Acknowledgements

Even sometimes life as an adult, your suffering may not come to an end. It is my hope that this story will not only bring forth conviction, but also bring correction to many parents.

My life as an adult has had its ups and downs, but I thank God for my trials and tribulations. Because without them, I couldn't have become the person that I am today.

I trust in God that my suffering has now come to a minimum.

First off, I want to thank God.

A special thanks to my children, Tieshia, Jeffrey, Jamarr, Jessica, Terrell, Otis and Keyshawn who were there for me through good and bad times, thank you. I love you all.

I definitely want to thank my Godmother Yvette Garlington for instilling positive values in me when it counted. I will never forget her beautiful face, may she rest in peace.

I also want to thank my Godpapa William Brown a.k.a (Dub) for inspiring me with his wisdom and love. I will never forget his generosity and I will always seek to bless others as he blessed me.

Endless love to my siblings.

Last but not least, my best friend, my love, a man that has shown me what love truly feels like, Cleon Sledge... I salute him for supporting and assisting me in the rebirth of The Bruises from my Mother's Love.

Hope you all enjoy...

Happy reading...!

Introduction

You're about to indulge yourself in a series of stories about my life. Some things you may find funny and some you may find disgraceful and other things I'm still waiting on words to describe them.

These incidents occurred as a young child while I was living at home with my mother.

You ever heard somebody say that the shit that happened to them was like a scene out of a movie? Well, they must have had me in mind when they made that statement. Because the way my mother treated me was more like a scene out of a horror movie.

This is an emotional story, believe me, each incident has something to offer your heart and your soul, so hold them both close as I take you on this emotional rollercoaster ride so you can see the highs and mostly lows of my early life.

CHAPTER 1

Our family, if you could call it that, was made up of my mother, Veronica, my little brother, Donte and myself, Lunye'; oh and sometimes my father, Jerry. He was there whenever he felt like being there.

I was my mother's first born and my father's second seed. I say seed because he was a seed layer, not a father. He was my mother's high school sweetheart and for some reason, she worshiped the ground he walked on. As for him, I don't know what his definition of love was, but I do know that together, they might as well have invented the phrase "dysfunctional couple."

We lived in an apartment on the west side of Chicago. It was a small apartment; to my brother and me it was like a mansion because we were so tiny. My mother was a beautiful light skinned black woman with long black hair, and she stood about five foot five and weighed about one hundred and twenty pounds. Her eyes were the shape of large almonds and she had the perfect face. When she did smile she lit up a room like Christmas lights shining in a dark room. Wow was she beautiful but had the attitude of an angry pit bull.

My father Jerry was about five foot eight and about one hundred and fifty pounds; he wore a low haircut and was very popular with the ladies--as they say, a "Ladies Man". He was always dressed to impressed and said all the right things to hypnotize the ladies.

People don't give children enough credit. They understand more than you know. We were young, but we had a lot of common sense, and we saw things we shouldn't have seen going on in our household, things like constant fighting, cussing and arguing. Whenever Jerry showed up, their arguments would start and the beatings would follow. I don't know why my mother put up with that kind of abuse. I only know his behavior only gave rise to countless beatings for me. The more he beat her, the more she hated and abused me.

Beautiful as my mother was, she always carried the meanest look on her face. That look that meant, *I will beat your ass if you say anything to me.*

They were both blessed with above average looks, but the thing they lacked was any ability to express love for their children. Not to mention quality parenting skills.

My mother only was seventeen when she had me and my father was nineteen. Maybe they were too young to have kids, but hey, shit happens (I guess.)

I will tell you this, the memories of their mistakes will last me a lifetime.

I know my mom was a woman that worked a lot but I don't remember my father working too much. If he did it was a secret.

I do remember how he used to beat my mom up and take her paycheck. Then he would go and hangout with his friends and other women and spend her money.

One time, when my father and mother were still together, my brother and I had a night of fun and laughter, we were awakened by shouting and cursing.

My mother was upset because my father wanted to take her paycheck from her for himself and I guess she wanted to put up a fight. The more she raised her voice the more he raised his. It was then that it got to the point that when my dad got tired of shouting and just started using his fists to do the talking and shouting for him.

We were told to stay in our room whenever they fought. I don't know if it was because she didn't want us to see them fight or what she was protecting us from him. I know one thing from the smell of the blood in the air I can always tell how bad my dad beat my mother. I know that sounds weird but my nose had some type of superpowers because any smell that my nose would encounter it would remember.

He used to beat my mother so bad, there were times when even I felt sorry for her.

Soon after the shouting had stopped, all you could hear was the front door slamming and the sniffles from my mother crying.

I had gotten out of my bed to go and see if she was okay. But when I'd asked her, she told me to get the hell out of her face. That was the last time I ever checked on her after my father beat her but it was incidents like this that was the reason why my father wasn't in our lives at this point.

I remember the next morning we were sitting at the table getting ready to eat breakfast right before school. My mom was quiet and she didn't say a word to us. As we sat in silence my brother made a funny face at me and I began to laugh. I tried to cover my mouth to stop myself from laughing but it wasn't fast enough.

I don't know what happened, but I think she thought that we were laughing at her or something because she hauled off and slapped the hell out of me; I fell out of my chair onto the floor and saw lightning.

My brother sat there in disbelief. She told him to get up and go to school. It was like my brother was running for his life. This was one of those times when you didn't have to force him to get to school on time because he was glad to leave. I, on the other hand, had to stay a little bit longer to finish up my beating. She took a cooking utensil and beat me on my back with it; while calling me names and asking did I think it was funny what my father had done to her.

I cried out saying, "No momma, no, I wasn't laughing at you."

In her head it was registering that I was laughing at her, so I said nothing and just finished taking my beating like a strong little girl. When she got done, she told me to go to school and tell all my friends how funny the ass whooping I just got was.

It gets even crazier, I found out later I even had a sister from another woman who was born just thirty days apart from me. She was born in June and I was born in July.

My father was a rolling stone but for some odd reason, my mother still wanted to be with him.

As the years went on, my father's beatings towards my mother escalated to the point my mother finally got up and left him.

We moved into another apartment, and I think she must have had very little money because that place had rats the size of newborn babies running around.

But she kept it clean, considering the building was bogus. In fact, she insisted on it. House cleaning was probably the first thing I learned how to do. She'd even stand me on a kitchen chair to do the dishes before I could reach the sink! But I learned very early to avoid getting hit, you did what she told you to do, exactly the way she wanted it done. My mom even cleaned the hallway because it led to our apartment. When you walked into that hallway, it smelled like bleach and Pine-sol.

Somewhere down the line she met this guy named Kenny, who worked for a toy company. He would just bring us toys for no reason and he would also hang out with us because he was a family type man. I don't know if I liked him or not, but I did like the toys, and things quieted down when he was around. At least for awhile.

After some time, my mother got pregnant with Kenny's baby. This kind of pissed me off because I could see the change in the way she treated us. It was almost as if she wished we had never been born.

So we moved again, into another apartment, I had to have been about seven to nine years old and my brother was about four or five years old. So here we were, in this one bedroom apartment. My brother and I shared the dining room as if it was a bedroom, which was fine with me just as long as we had a roof over our heads.

My mother's pregnancy was a horrible ordeal. The unnecessary beatings and verbal abuse was beginning to get out of control. I even thought maybe that's how women act when they were pregnant. How was I to know any better?

She gave birth to a baby girl named Deonna. She was a cute baby and when my mom brought her home I thought to myself, that I finally got somebody besides Donte to play with. But the baby soon turned into a headache because I had to hold her bottles and change her diapers and watch her all day. I had no choice; that was the way Mama wanted it.

I remember one time when I was watching Deonna and I didn't know any better, I saw her trying to slide off the couch. I thought she was trying to walk on her own.

I really thought it was a cool thing so I ran up to my mother's friend's house to get her, so she could see.

She told me "Bitch, if my baby fell off that couch I'm fucking you up".

In the back of my mind, I was asking God to please not let her fall and sure enough, when we were walking through the door, I heard my little sister screaming at the top of her lungs.

At that point I was pretty sure my life was over. Deonna was on the floor. My mother ran over to pick her up and laid her back down.

When suddenly, it's like I heard a herd of horses coming towards me. All I could do was assume the position and just wait for it.

The position was like a karate move or something but even that never worked. I always walked away with a black eye or some type of bruise. She kept her word. She beat the fuck out me. She busted my lip, blackened my eye and called me every name but the child of God.

There was only one thing to do afterward; wait until she left and then call her names and tell God on her. I didn't know much about God. I was introduced to his name by hearing other children saying "I swear to God." Without asking, I assumed from their gestures that he was someone that was really great and he was someone that had great powers. I don't think my mother feared God, but I had to hold on to something to keep me going. Unlike others, my mother never showed a spiritual side; she did go to church a time or two on Easter but was never involved in church.

Months down the line, she had the nerve to get pregnant again. I couldn't understand it. It wasn't as though she showed any sign at all of loving her children. Most of the time, it was more like she wanted us dead. Besides, she could have given me a heads up, considering I was the damn nanny without pay.

So here we go again. Another damn sibling and more beatings to come. On top of that, her attitude got worse when she was pregnant. I was feeling like Cinderella.

My brother would just sit back and play with his army men and try to stay out of the way, but the one thing he couldn't dodge was those ass whippings when she wanted to feed her demon.

For him, the whippings weren't that bad because he was still pretty young and fragile. Sometimes my thoughts would wander and I would imagine just grabbing my little brother and running away. Then reality would kick in and remind me that I am only a kid myself with no money and nowhere to go.

Another damn baby is here and we already didn't have enough room for us. Well at least she kept it clean. Or shall I say I kept it clean?

She had another baby girl by the name of Desire. She was such a cute little thing, but she was so hairy, I loved her anyways.

Now that we had a new addition to the family, there were also more problems.

Well for me that is, because I had to change diapers, make bottles, baby sit, get ass whippings and I had to clean up.

So, if I had to sum it all up, I would say that I was a slave.

Now there were four kids and two adults. Well, actually it was one adult. Kenny stopped coming over right around when Desire was born. I really believe he left because he just couldn't deal with the dysfunction inside of our household. It was almost like he was able to see pass her pretty face and he saw her true identity. I thanked God my mother was letting the girls sleep in the bed with her because that gave me and my brother time to bond.

As time went on and the girls got bigger, mine and my brother's space was no longer our own. And the whole while, it became clearer and clearer how much my mother favored her younger babies over Donte and me.

After Kenny stopped coming over, a new sheriff came to town. His name was Henry and he was a cop. For some reason, I was relieved to know that.

Unlike Kenny, Henry would even step in and tell my mom to stop hitting on us and calling us names. I remember telling God thank you for sending us someone to protect us.

My mom was a very smart and manipulative woman, she would simply wait for him to leave, and then she would beat us.

One day, she blackened my eye again and put bruises all over me because I didn't wash the dishes correctly. She would always try to tell me to go to bed early before Henry got there, but this time, he saw me peeping from under the covers.

That's when he came over and starts tickling me. When he saw my eye, he immediately called my mother into the other room. When they went into the other room, I was so afraid I didn't even eavesdrop on their conversation.

I know when they came out of the room he made my mom apologize to me. Although I won the victory, I lost the war because I knew he had to leave again and I wished that I could've gone with him.

Henry ended up staying the night that night and the girls had to sleep with us. It made me mad I guess, but I was so grateful that he didn't leave I couldn't even get too angry, even though the girls got on my nerves all night.

When morning came and Henry was about to leave, I looked at him as if he wasn't never coming back. She must have had a good night because when he left she didn't mention nothing about the night before, she just told me to mop the floor.

Henry and my mother's relationship progressed and then it was time for us to move on. We moved to a new neighborhood with no warning. It was not too far from the neighborhood that we resided in, it was a step up from what we where use to all because there were no roaches or mice. As we approached the new neighborhood I remember the smell of fresh cut grass and barbeque which caused a hunger pain in my stomach. I remember the sound of children's feet thumping on the concrete from running and the sound of their laughter tickled my ears, forcing me to smile momentarily.

It was a one bedroom apartment with a living room and dining room which we used as a bedroom as well. My living arrangements weren't exactly what I would call "little house on the prairie-style".

This was no fairytale. While it's true that I had a mother and father figure in the same household for once, but what did I profit from it? I got nothing but bad memories and holes in my heart that have yet to heal.

They say that when kids grow up in a home with an absent father or a single parent the chances of them having a normal life when they get older will be slim.

If you ask me, I think they need to do another study. Because I've had both and my life and was more hell growing up than I'd wish on anyone.   We soon moved to another apartment, but that was after my sisters got bigger and we needed the space. We ended up in a Hispanic neighborhood "Humboldt Park". The neighborhood looked really nice and there where children hanging out on the block and the sound of their laughter gave me hope. The building was a two-flat; we would be residing on the second floor which had an attic attached to it.

This new place we considered big because we had two bedrooms now, so we all slept in that one room with bunk beds and my mom slept in the other bedroom just down the hall.

This kind of gave us a little bit more space because this one had a larger living room, dining room and kitchen and it was well kept.

Then again, there was no reason for it not to be because my mother had me and my brother cleaning it from top to bottom all the time. Notice, I said me and my brother, it was never my other two sisters Deonna and Desire.

I thought that they never helped out because they were smaller but even as we all got bigger they still never helped me and my brother with household chores. Now I see that it was because my mother was favoring them.

I grew to hate sharing a room with them because they never respected mine and my brother's things.

Sure, we all shared this bedroom but they treated our room like it was theirs, all because they had the most toys and clothes.

There were times when my brother and I felt like visitors in our own room. We couldn't touch anything that belonged to them, nor could we play with their toys. My mother would beat us half to death if we put our hands on anything that belonged to my sisters but it was always okay for them to play with everything we owned. She treated them different because they had a different dad than my little brother and I.

I wish that I could give an excuse for my mother abusing my brother and me the way she did but I can't, I can only tell it like it was.

I remember the time when I was a little girl and I had caught a cold. Now this is the time when a five year old needs her mother's tender love and care.

My mother didn't and wouldn't do a damn thing to soothe me. Whenever it was time for me to take my medicine she used to pour the cough syrup in a spoon that I thought was kind of big for the dosage that I needed and shoved it into my mouth like she hated the fact that I was sick, or better yet, that she had to take care of me.

She didn't give me my medicine like a loving mother should. She practically shoved the spoon to the back of my throat.

The way she did it made me cough harder because the medicine burned the back of my throat.

My mother got mad because as I was coughing a little bit of the medicine came out of my mouth and it splattered on her blouse. She hit me in my face and told me to watch what the hell I was doing and I was supposed to cover my mouth when I coughed. Well hey, she never taught me that, so how was I supposed to know to cover my mouth when I coughed? I was still at a learning stage.

I was five years old at that time and she treated me like I'm supposed to know the same things as a thirteen year old. Yet, she didn't want to take the time to teach me anything. Maybe if I have been born into the world already knowing right from wrong, she would have been satisfied just so she didn't have to take the time to teach me anything.

For as long as I can remember, my mom treated us like we were enemies from her past because my brother and I had the same father and different from my two younger sisters. Was it because our father abused her and my other sisters' father didn't? I think it was me in particular that she didn't like the most. She treated me like I was public enemy number one.

There were times when I'd be playing with my toys and I would look up at her and she would give me this look of disgust. Like I was that bitter taste in her mouth.

Me being a child, I never understood why she would look at me like that, but it sure wasn't the look of love. I can remember as far back to when I was about three years old when we were having a bar-be-que and my mom was fussing at me for something, I can't quite remember, but she went to lash out at me and I ran from her.

I was too busy trying to keep my eye on her and run at the same time that I ended up running into the grill and burned my arm.

You would think her response would have been "Baby are you alright?"

Hell no, it was, "See that's what your little ass get trying to run from me."

She then told me to go sit my ass down somewhere.

This was just one of many ass whippings I got. I can remember a time when I was about six years old or younger when my mother beat me for about fifteen minutes or more. I can't recall what happened or what I had done to her, but it was almost as if I was the other woman that stole her man or something 'cause she beat me like I was a stranger on the street.

It felt like I was in a street fight the way she screamed at me and put scratches all over me. I tried my best to protect my face as she beat me repeatedly.

I can still smell the stench of her breath from her spitting in my face as she was yelling at me, the blood that poured from my nose and mouth as she beat me while calling me names that were a disgrace to human nature.

I just kept saying to myself that I wish she would get tired so that the pain can stop already but it was mostly the emotional and mental abuse that hurt the worst.

It was in that moment that I knew that my life as a young child was going to be a painful one. I mean the verbal abuse and the nasty looks she gave me hurt more than being whipped with an extension cord, which I've been beaten with as well.

I couldn't imagine why a mother would have such hate in her heart for her child. I'd always question myself as to what led up to this hate. I couldn't ever come up with an answer, but I believe the abuse stemmed from my father.

Sometimes I think my friends knew that I was getting beat because there were times when I went to school and couldn't play, sit or jump rope with them. I truly never knew their thoughts but from the looks on their faces they were disturb by my appearance.

Though they looked at me funny, I played it off as though my brother and I were playing too rough at home. Maybe my teachers noticed, too. However, they never asked too many questions, I guess maybe I was a good liar or maybe they just didn't care.

I'd never open my mouth about my mother beating my brother and I, we feared her too much to say anything to anyone. Time went on and of course the beatings, the verbal abuse and other types of abuse in all areas continued, they also got worse. Yet it was just the beginning to a long childhood of misery.

CHAPTER 2

The rumbling in my stomach woke me up in the middle of the night. I was a growing girl and sometimes the amount of food we were given at dinner time wasn't enough to fill me up, so I'd sneak into the kitchen and get food out of the refrigerator. I'd tiptoe to the kitchen, open the fridge and take a few pieces of leftover chicken that my mother cooked for us earlier that day, put some ketchup on it and go back to my room and eat.

After I got done I wanted some water so bad but didn't want to chance getting caught. I may have gotten away with going to get the food but I might not get away with going back for water. I thought to myself, just maybe I can be quiet like I was the first time, so again I got out of my bed and walked to the kitchen. I didn't even let the water run…. matter of fact I didn't even let the water hit the sink because

I just knew that the sound of the water splashing would be heard.

So I turned the water on enough for it to trickle into my hand as I controlled the pressure with my other hand. I stood on my tip toes and drank for a few seconds. Then I turned the water off and hurried back to my room.

Just as I got to our bedroom door my brother peeked out of the room. "I'm hungry, too," he said. I knew he was. Like I said, our mother never fed us enough to get full.

As always, I felt obligated to get it for him because he was hungry as well. Above all, I was willing to take a beating for him because he was my brother. As much as I hated it, I turned to go back while he watched for my mother.

By the time I reached the kitchen to retrieve my brother's food, he saw our mother come out of her room. He got so scared; he immediately closed the bedroom door in fear. As my mother walked to the bathroom, my brother peeked through the slightly opened door, waiting to give me a signal that my mother was awake and I should be careful.

Just as I was coming down the hallway my mom snatched me by the back of my head with a hand full of my hair.

"What the hell are you doing out of bed? Think you can get away with stealing my food? Huh?HUH?" She made it clear that I didn't buy nothing in the refrigerator and I shouldn't be in it taking anything out. The chicken that I got for my brother fell to the floor while she roughed me up, slapping me and pulling my hair.

When she saw that the food had fallen on the floor she got even angrier. It was like the devil had released his wife upon me. It's like she was out of her body or something. I screamed for mercy as she led me around the floor by my ponytails, telling me to pick the chicken up. She barely bent me down enough to reach the food, so I stretched the best way I could to pick up the chicken but the further I reached, the more my hair pulled from my scalp. She then accused me of not trying to pick the food up off the floor.

So she slammed me down to the floor and told me to finish the food since I was so hungry and bold enough to steal. What she didn't know was that I had eaten already and I was full. She made me eat that chicken off the floor. As I sat there crying, I wasn't sure whether she was beating me for crying or for taking the food.

She made me feel ashamed for eating when I was hungry. She also made me sit there on the floor until I got done eating the chicken. I was getting sick because I was still full from eating minutes before. I gagged on it but my mother dared me to throw up.

That was the longest meal I had ever eaten. It was like the more I ate the more chicken appeared for me to eat. I could hear my brother in our room crying because he felt at fault that I was being beaten.

No matter if he told my mother that the food was for him she still beat me. That nearly endless nightmare finally ended with her leading me to our bedroom by my hair.

She threw me inside and said, "Take your ass to bed, and you better get up on time for school." Little did she know was that I could never wait for school because that was like a mini vacation from Hell.

School was the only time that I felt free to laugh, smile, talk and be myself. I took that time to kind of reinvent myself from what my mother was trying to turn me into. Some of the things I did as a child were things that most children my age did and they all may have gotten whippings over it but I don't think they got beat for it. At least not the way I did. My mother raised us different; we were "well kept" kids. My mother camouflaged our abuse very well because she kept us well dressed and very clean. I believe that she really thought that made her a good parent. But it did make strangers think she was a good parent, but she could hide it from the people that knew her well.

Everyone would always say Veronica have some very well-mannered children, that's because the fear of my mother's beating kept us in line. It was bittersweet because of course, kids are supposed to be well behaved. Most times

I believed my mom loved me with her fist and hated me with her heart. I believe that even grown men couldn't endure the beatings my mother gave me. A few times, I was sure I was just going to die.

Other times, I actually wished that I was dead just to escape the beatings and verbal abuse my mother pierced me with. I lived in fear my whole childhood. It was never normal, I didn't, nor was I allowed to do the normal things other kids were able to do, like go outside and play, because if I did, there was always a problem. Like I was laughing too much or I was just having too much fun and believe it or not, I got beat for that, too. I mean, that's how she made me.

Some nights when I wasn't sleeping, I would ask God what I did to deserve such misery of course I never got an answer. I always tried to be a good child. I'd look after my brother and do my chores.

I mean, we did everything my mother asked and we always got the short end of the stick anyway. Honestly, it would be times we would come to our house, filled with the fragrance of fried chicken, gravy and rice with biscuits and boy, we couldn't wait until dinner, only to sit at the table with a big bowl of pork and beans with hot dogs cut up inside. Believe me, this was not when Christmas, Thanksgiving, Easter, and all those types of holiday dinners were going on we didn't see food from them. If our grandmother or aunties didn't make it happen we'd be ass out. Let's not leave out birthdays; we barely knew what that was unless she wanted to show off for her friends or the family.

Every holiday and birthday was like Halloween…it was Hell. That's why I laid in my bed, praying that those days would end soon There were times when I'd wish that I could just wake up and be grown already and just skip the whole kid thing. That way, I could just walk out the front door and be free and never look back. I was young and I had a long way to go before that happened.

On my birthday, she never went all out for me. My birthday was just another day she felt wasn't important enough to celebrate. I believe I may have had maybe one or two birthday parties that I do remember. I'm sure they were not for me; they were for a front to look like a good mommy. To make matters worse, I couldn't even go outside and play with my friends. All I was able to do was stay in the house, clean and fetch things for her while she either talked on the phone to her friends or watched television. After about seven or eight years, I stopped counting and expecting anything for my birthday, and my brother's birthdays were as dreadful as mine.

Like I said, we both just stopped looking forward to those days. Now when my sisters came around, boy, was that a different story. My brother and I watched as our mother practically saved money to give our little sisters Deonna and Desire a good birthday party. There was nothing that my brother and I could do but attend. The same happened on Christmas.

It just goes to show you how much I mattered in my mother's life.

I wasn't important enough to have a birthday party every year,

I wasn't important enough to get anything for Christmas and I really wasn't important enough for her to care when I was being abused and at times, not even by her hands.

I mean, I was really going through some stuff as a child and didn't have my mother there emotionally to care for me. Now you might say what could a child that's eight, nine, and ten years old be going through? Trust me, I was going through enough to make the Pope scream.

I'm telling you if I could cash in on all the bullshit I went through as a child and I mean before the age of thirteen I'd probability be the richest kid in America.

CHAPTER 3

My mother was out with one of her friends that lived in our building. The sun was shining and it was a beautiful day; the neighborhood kids were all outside playing and as usual I watched from our window. They had looks of freedom and happiness on their faces as they played games with each other. I pretended that I was there with them- running up and down the street, while my brother and the other kids tried to catch me in a game of tag.

I was in such a daze that I didn't see my mother come in and being in the windows in our house was a no-no. I never understood why she didn't approve of us not opening the window and looking out but she made it clear that I was not to open her window or doors. She always gave rules but without explanation. I remember her giving me a lecture about how she felt about us being in the window as I watched her unplug the television and other appliances to get the extension cord. Seeing her come toward me with that cord in her hand scared me senseless. I felt my life as I knew it was over. So I tensed my body up and squeezed my eyes shut tight so I wouldn't see the whipping coming.

The first time she struck me with the cord, it hurt but not as much as I thought it would. I think she knew it too, that's why she told me to get undressed. Lord knows I didn't want to take my clothes off and endure this beating but things would only get worse if I didn't. I thought I could slow the beating down by procrastinating, so I began to peel my clothes away slowly. She hit me with the cord to make me take them off faster and that was enough fire for me. No matter how bad I screamed for her mercy, and pleaded for her to stop, it only registered in her brain as though I was begging for her to hit me harder. It went on until she wore herself out.

The lashes on my naked body blistered and bled. They burned with pain and sizzled with heat from my body temperature. Whenever my mom got done beating me there was never any remorse for what she had done. She would look at my wounds as though they were her trophies or something; she never took the blame. Though I was already hurting she still slapped and punched me for bleeding on the floor or for making her have to bandage me up afterward. This particular time, she ran warm water in the tub with some witch hazel for the swelling. She made me sit in and soak for about thirty minutes or so.

This was the one time I didn't want to sit or sleep. It hurt too badly.

I was in so much pain it took my breath away. I had to brace myself while walking through the house because I didn't want nothing or no one to bump against me. I didn't even want the clothes on my back. If I could have walked around the house naked I would have just so my clothes wouldn't be irritating to my cuts from the extension cord she had whipped me with. Its times like this I wished for death or for someone to save us. It's just unreal for a mother to beat her own child the way she did me.

I must have been taking the beatings for all the kids in the world, because every time I saw kids around me they seemed so happy, like they didn't get whipped like I did, but then again I don't think any kids got the beatings I received I was so young but had the cuts and bruises of a person that had lived a great amount of years. I was hiding bumps and bruises at the ages of five, six and seven years old, and they only got worse.

How loud does a child really have to cry to get their pain soothed, their bruises pampered and the cuts mended? I could have been sitting in the midst of a crowd and it's like no one heard my cries for freedom. People back in those days didn't quite get in other people's business anyway. Or they could have known what was going on with me but just didn't give a damn. There were a few that really didn't know because we were so well kept. People have a funny way of seeing only what they want to see.

Some just couldn't see my mother doing anything wrong. They used to say that what goes on in the home stays in the home, but what if what's going on in the home is wrong and needed to be corrected? Each and every day children are being abused and it goes on without notice, because people choose to either look the other way or they just don't want to get involved. All while this is happening, kids are being neglected and abused and a very high percentage of them are dying in the process.

I have cried so many tears there should be a river named after me somewhere. As a child I don't think I ever cried tears of joy, they were always tears of fear, sadness, pain and loneliness. I use to think maybe it was the tone of my dark skin that was the reason why my mother hated me so much but I was too young to even try and define actually why she treated me as bad as she did. My mother did work a lot she worked at a liquor store, but she also wasn't the type that got drunk and passed out leaving her children to fend for themselves it's almost like she enjoyed making me suffer by her hands the most.

That's one of the reasons why I couldn't figure out why she was so damn mean to us, me and my brother in particular. I mean, she wasn't a drinker and she didn't do drugs, so what was her reason for beating us the way she did? It was like it was a mystery. No one talked much about it in our family because everyone was segregated.

When she was at work that was the best time ever! She'd never leave us alone while she worked. My auntie, who lived upstairs, used to look in on us from time to time. Well, she wasn't really my aunt; she was my mom's long time friend. We just called her our aunt.

Other times she would have our Uncle James to watch us; at least I thought he was our uncle. He'd come over with ice cream and junk food for everybody, more so for me. He would bring me money, too, along with pops, chips, and everything. We loved when he came because that was one of the few times when we could have a little freedom to eat what we wanted to. I wondered why he would give me more than the other kids. He watched us on several occasions. It turned suddenly, he was doing more than babysitting. He was watching me in a different way. He would have me clean up when everybody was asleep. Then he would wait until everybody went to sleep and come in my room and wake me up to wash the dishes or something. I did try and do them while everybody was awake, but he used to make up a story about how we were kids and we needed to play. "Clean up later", he would say.

Later, when everyone was asleep, it was just me and him. I remember standing at the sink washing the dishes. I was trying to hurry up so I could get back into my bed before he came in there with me. He approached me from behind and said, "Slow down, why you going so fast?" He then helped me wash the dishes as he stood behind me. He stood so close that I could feel him brushing his manhood up against my butt as he sniffed my hair, breathing hard in my ear. Then, he took his wet, soapy hands and rubbed them up and down my arms.

"See? Don't that feel better? It's much more fun when you take your time and just play in the soap."

Talk about feeling uncomfortable, I'm not sure what or who he thought I was, but he was treating me like a woman that was ready to start doing some pretty grown up things.

I felt so dirty and ashamed. I thought I should tell my mom that my uncle touched, but somehow I felt responsible. Besides, my mom always made me feel like I was the one that did things wrong, so I kept it to myself. Maybe this is how it was supposed to be. I was taught nothing about things like sex. It made me angry though, because I know if it felt wrong, then it was wrong. All I had was my common sense to rely on.

When he sent me to my room, I lay in my bed, using the sheets to wipe my face and around my neck, trying to get the smell of his cologne off of me. I didn't know whether to tell my mom or not; she made me feel so bad about everything else I was for sure that she was going to blame me for what happened.

Knowing my mother she'd say that I was being fresh with him and that I pushed myself upon him. I felt so alone and scared, but since I didn't know any better, I just learned to go with the flow and keep quiet. It seemed like when I did this, I got fewer beatings. I really believe I became a target because he knew my mother was abusing me and he knew I was too scared to tell.

A few nights after that first incident, my mom was working a night shift and she had Uncle James to watch us again. He sat on the couch watching me put our toys away. He told my brother and sisters to go in their rooms and play. I was confused when he told me to come and sit on his lap. He talked dirty to me as if I was fulfilling a fantasy of his or something.

He talked about my hair and the way I looked in my gown at bedtime. Though I had quite a figure for my age I think that's what attracted him to touch me the way he did. Either way, it wasn't appropriate. So he sat me down on his knee and began to make his knee vibrate between my legs while grinding my private area at the same time. Whenever he got done, he was always out of breath, tired and weak I didn't know what that meant. I just know that when it happened, he always would tell me to go to my room as if he couldn't bear to look at me after that. The next day, when I came in from school he was there again. He called me over, saying that he was sorry, then he kissed me. Somewhat like a man kissing and making up with his girlfriend. I felt so disgusted and uncomfortable. And I knew he wasn't sorry because he'd always do it again.

This went on for quite some time. I don't know what happened to my Uncle James but after while, he never came around again.

Now that I had reached eleven years old, I was told to watch my younger brother and sisters and if anything was to happen to them or the house I was going to get the beating of my life, but hell, I felt like I was already getting those.

One night, my mom was working and my sisters were playing through the house and ended up breaking a lamp. They threw something and made the lamp turn over, causing the light bulb to blow out. I was so upset because I knew that I was going to have to pay for it. So I told them to go to their rooms and of course they gave me back talk and told me that they were gonna tell my mother that I hit them. This was their way of getting my mother to beat me. They always used this method against me and it always worked. When they wanted to get me into trouble, they would lie to my mom and tell her that I hit them just so I would get a whipping. Even they knew she treated us different, it was me and my brother Donte against them. Nothing like a house divided.

So anyway, they broke the light bulb on the living room lamp. After I made them to go bed, I stayed up trying to fix it. Even when I changed the bulb, nothing happened. I was getting frustrated because it almost time for her to come home and the lamp still wasn't working. So I hid it behind the couch and hoped that maybe when she came home, she'd just go to bed and I could fix it in the morning. Or so I thought. It didn't happen; my mother came in, tossed her coat on the couch and reached for the lamp to turn the light on.

She asked, "Where the hell is the lamp?"

I couldn't do anything but stand there and look confused, as though I didn't know what she was talking about. She knew this because she was like, "don't stand there looking dumb and shit, where the hell the lamp at?"

I told her what happened, that my sisters were playing when I was cleaning the up kitchen and they knocked it over. She accused me of letting them tear up the house while she was at work. She then said that it was probably me and my brother Donte broke it. My mom never thought that my sisters did anything wrong. And of course I got my ass beat for that lamp.

CHAPTER 4

My brother was a sweet little boy, he was my heart and I always felt the need to protect him. We got the same amount of beatings and for the same petty things practically, but in some way she always managed to beat me the worst. I will never forget one time when my brother got a whipping for making what we called, sugar water.

That's when you mix sugar and water together to make a sweet drink to substitute for something you wish you had, like, Kool-Aid or juice. To us, it was the best and enjoyable drink we had next to nothing but my mother hated when we messed with her sugar. We weren't allowed to touch nothing in the house without her permission. Even when we asked, the answer was always no. So one day my brother came in from playing outside and he was thirsty. He went to the kitchen and made himself a glass of sugar water. My mom was next door talking to one of the neighbors.

As I looked on, I prayed that my mother would stay gone until he got finished. But my brother took too long; he always took too long doing something. Me, being the oldest, I kind of had this radar thing where I knew when my mother was coming and as long as my brother took, I just knew she was on her way back. Just as I went into the kitchen to tell him to hurry up, there she was, standing there and ready for war. We both stood in fear as we saw our lives flashing before us.

The look on her face was a familiar one. At least I had seen it many times and I already knew what was about to happen. She looked at us and said that we were trying to steal from her. She called us thieves and accused us of plotting to disobey her, together. Her mind was always in overdrive. She thought that we were the ones that were out to get her or we were to blame for her life turning out the way it did. It had to be something to make her see red every time she saw us. I thought for sure that I was gonna get beat for this. But when she told me to get out the way and for my brother to take his clothes off, my heart dropped I lost my breath as my heart raced because I knew what her whippings did to me, but it was another thing for my brother because he was small. His body just wouldn't have been able to take it.

As I turned to walk away, my brother wept in fear, so I tried to convince her that it was me that made the sugar water for him, and that I was at fault but she wasn't buying it. When my brother took off his clothes she took her cord and whacked him across the front of his little body. His screams made me feel helpless.

I ran to my room and hid in a corner and poked my fingers in my ears so I wouldn't hear him screaming. As she beat him, she preached to him about doing things without her permission. She also accused him of following in my footsteps by going in the kitchen getting food to eat like we bought it. She always compared his wrongdoing to mine which gave me reason to believe she was beating him while thinking of me. She couldn't come up with a legitimate reason to whip me so she used his wrongdoing as an excuse but she always managed to make it about me.

So after my brother's whipping, she called me into the living room and told me that I was about to get beat for trying to lie about me making the sugar water so that my brother wouldn't get in trouble.

So why was I getting a whipping? She said for lying.

Hmmmm, here we go again.

The things that were going through my head were out of this world.

I'm thinking, okay it is official; she really hates us, me in particular. My eyes filled with tears but they were no longer tears of fear, but of anger. It was becoming crystal clear to me that I wasn't her favorite person in the world. Nor would

I ever be. I can't even say child because she never treated me as such. So the feelings were becoming mutual. If she didn't love me as her child, then I couldn't bring myself to love her as my mother.

We had been beaten over some very petty things, but making something as simple as sugar water, our low budget drink, was just ridiculous.

We couldn't have the things other children had, so we found other ways to make ourselves happy. I mean, it wasn't like we had a loving mother or father to make us feel wanted, loved and refreshed. So my brother and I indulged ourselves in things that made us happy. They were simple but my mother made them major offenses.

As I stood there, waiting for my whipping, my mom always gave some half ass speech about what we did, but it never was what we did wrong. In some cases we didn't do anything, she just was finding reasons to release her hostile energy on us. I don't know what was worse, the wounds I examined after the whippings or the verbal abuse I had to endure, as if the beating didn't hurt enough.

She always had her way of making things hurt intensely whether they were words or objects. Trust me, if either one was in my mother's arsenal they were gonna hurt like hell; the name calling, and degrading words she spoke, the spitting in my face and the burns.

I mean, if this is what it was going to be like in this world with a mother loving you with hate, then I'd wish that she would have just aborted me.

Later that night, I nursed my little brother's wounds. The lashes on his body ached with agony as he cried and whined, calling my name telling me that his cuts burned. I pampered his wounds and told him that everything was going to be okay.

Every time my brother got a whipping I was always there to try and ease his pain. But there was something about our bond that made our mother upset. At times like this, we would stick together, and she couldn't understand why we didn't have that kind of bond with our other two sisters. Even though she had herself to thank for that, because when it came to us, she would always get in the middle and try to interfere.

She already treated them different from my brother Donte and me. When it came to some of the things that went wrong around the house, she should have known for a fact that it was one of my other sisters, Desire or Deonna, but only Donte or I would pay for it. We were starting to get used to it. Whippings around our house were becoming protocol; they were natural to me, and I learned to cry on the inside. The only time I cried out was when I was trying to get her to stop hitting me.

But as time went on, even that wasn't working, so I learned to endure it until she got tired. You would think that at the first sight of blood or pain that she'd stop, but it was almost as though our suffering gave her motivation to keep going.

I remember when my younger sister's father Jerry would come over with toys for us. He witnessed our mother hitting us on one occasion and totally disagreed. He asked why she would beat us to the extent to where we had bruises.

Her answer was, "These are my damn kids and I'm gonna whip they ass whenever and however I want."

She didn't beat us anymore, around Jerry that is.

She'd just wait until he left to whip us for whatever we didn't do.

One time when he came over and played with us, my brother must have said or did something that made my mother upset because she just slapped him. I don't quite remember what the incident was, but Jerry didn't like it one bit. This time I was sure that he was going to tell us to pack our stuff and leave with him.

That didn't happen!

He told my mother he didn't like the way she treated us and how she would beat us to the point we bled. Then he grabbed his coat and left without us.

I don't think that my soul has ever cried out as loud as it did that time. There were so many opportunities we had to leave, if only we had some help, but somehow we never got close to being gone for good.

We did have an auntie that used to take me over to her house to spend some nights, but my mom would always come up with some lame ass excuse about how I either didn't finish my chores or she had something for me to do, just so my auntie could bring me home.

Deep down, I knew it was because she just couldn't stand the thought that I was having fun. As a kid, fun was never in our vocabulary. Fun was what my brother and I made it. We couldn't be too loud about it either, or else we would have gotten beat for it.

Now I have taken some beatings not only for myself but also taken them for my brother. But there was one time he took a whipping for me.

I had come home from school on time and saw that my mom wasn't there so I went in the refrigerator and drank some milk. My mom always set things up so that she'd know when we went in the kitchen and messed with anything, so I tried to put the milk carton back the way I thought she had it.

When she came home, I heard her yelling, asking who went in the milk. My brother and I looked at each other. I told him that I was about to go tell her that I did it. He stopped me.

"I don't want you to tell her that. You still healing from your last ass whipping."

It was true. I still had a black eye from her last beating. So he went in there and told my mother that it was him that drank the milk. She told him to undress while she searched for something to whip him with. By the time my brother got out of his clothes, she couldn't find anything so she took her shoe off and beat him with the bottom of it.

My brother's screams went from apologetic to chanting as he bled. I've been around beatings long enough to know when someone was bleeding from the times when my father use to beat my mother to the times when my mother beat us. It was like my nose was keen to the smell of fresh blood. The scent of blood was in the air when she was beating my brother and I knew he wasn't lying, so I got up to peep out of my bedroom door and I saw her beating him as he bled from his head. She had hit Donte in his head with the heel of her shoe.

She didn't let up either. Once again, it was like she wasn't in her body. It was like an uncaring soul had entered without mercy because the sight of blood would make anybody stop beating someone. I just wished for that moment I was an adult so I could avenge him.

When my brother saw that she wasn't going to stop, he folded himself into a fetal position and stayed until she got tired.

She never checked to see if he was okay. When she got done she went in her room and shut the door. I ran to his aid, grabbing a towel to put pressure on his head. I couldn't apologize enough for what he just endured for me. I felt so bad but he wouldn't let me be sorry. He said that we were brother and sister and we had to stick together.

It wasn't until later on that night that my mother showed any concern for him.

When she saw that his head had an open gash, she sort of babied him, telling him that she was sorry and she was going to buy him something real nice. She told him that soon as Deonna and Desire's dad brought her some money she was going to go and buy him some junk especially for him. To me, it didn't sound like she was sincere; it was more of a guilt trip.

It took a long time for his head to heal because she never took him to the hospital for stitches. She just nursed it herself until it started to close on its own. And the longer his head took to heal, the longer the junk food and presents she promised him took getting to him.

When things smoothed over, she went back to her old self. When he asked our mother about the junk food she'd promised, she told him to get the fuck out of her face. She then blamed him for the trouble she had to go through to heal his head. So since he put her through that, she said, he wasn't getting nothing.

My brother didn't miss the message. I wasn't the only one to build a wall of hate for our mother. He was starting to build his own.

Sometimes I'd see the anger in his eyes. He hated being her child just like she hated being our mother. I could see him starting to become emotionless, numb to what was going on.

Maybe he was getting to be like me, used to the situation and adjusting to being abused. At our house, it was what they called "normal."

How does someone adjust to being beat all the time? Can you imagine waking up every day, knowing that you gonna get beat and mentally abused. Our minds were twisted up, thinking that hate was love and if that was the case, then we'd rather stay in a permanent sleep. It didn't take a rocket scientist to know that a mother's love wasn't the color of black and blue, nor was it supposed to feel like a fist of pain.

If someone were to ask me what was the meaning of love? I wouldn't be able to tell them, because that was not something that was ever talked about in our household, nor was it exercised.

When someone told me that they loved me, it made me feel uncomfortable; it felt more like they were calling me out and I knew it was better to stay invisible. I used to hang my head low when people said that to me, because I always felt that love was a bad thing, especially when it was said and or expressed.

My mother didn't even take the time to explain what the difference was between good love and bad love. She didn't even tell me what to do if people tried to touch me in my private areas. So I didn't know whether to tell or not, because every time I opened my mouth I got beat, so if someone did me harm I was too afraid to tell. My mom already made me feel that everything was my fault, so if somebody did something to me, I couldn't help but to think that it was my fault. And my fault always equaled a beating.

CHAPTER 5

At this point in my life, when I was 12 or 13 years old, I was becoming someone else. Someone that needed to break away from this monstrous tale of terror that took place in my so-called home. Every day, I began taking detours after school just so I could get a moment of peace. There were some kids from my school that started hanging out at this girl's house because no one was never home during school hours. That was the place to be.

We would dance, play, laugh and have fun. Sometimes, we would just watch TV and talk. When we shared stories, my friend's stories about their houses and how their mother treated them were way different from mine.

They complained about how they had to take out the garbage and wash dishes. If they didn't, they would get their phone and TV privileges taken from them.

I laughed on the inside. I didn't even know what the hell a phone privilege was. It was like they were speaking a different language.

When they did something wrong at home, they got things taken from them like toys, phone and TV time and also not being able to go outside and play. I didn't know whether to laugh or be mad.

I wished all my mother did was take a luxury item from me when I did something wrong. Instead, I got my freedom, childhood, and security of my parents taken away, along with a long list of other things. Whenever it was my turn to tell some of the things my mom did that made me angry. I would just laugh it off, as I shrugged my shoulders and agreed with whatever they said about their parents. I could have had them there all day and night talking about the things I went through with my mother.

I'll tell you what; I bet they wouldn't complain as much if I was to tell them what really happened to me when I even think about some of the stuff they did to get in trouble.

I'd just sit back and admire them though. The truth was, they had all the things I wanted.

I'm not speaking about luxury items, either. I'm saying that I wished that I had the freedom to go outside and play. I was a little more than a slave. Only slaves aren't allowed to complain, if they do, they're severely punished.

Whenever I'm thirsty I want to be able to go in the fridge and get a drink of water. When I just need a hug, it would be nice to be able to walk up to my mother and just get one. Just so that I can feel loved and protected.

I envied my friends for having those types of privileges. Those things were a luxury to me, not toys, clothes or candy. Maybe they knew I was different, but I don't think they ever suspected the truth. They even used to talk about how I used to wear my clothes. Some days when it was warm or hot outside I would wear long sleeve shirts and pants. They thought it was because I was just weird like that.

If they only knew. The long sleeves and pants were my way of hiding the bruises that I suffered from getting beat for the things they took for granted. They just don't know how bad I wanted to just strip out of my clothes and show them what a real ass whipping looked like and what the side effects were. Maybe they would've appreciated their parents more. Hell, sometimes I wish it was just that simple, to get put in a corner just because I didn't take out the garbage.

One day, the time was getting away from us and it was time for us to all make our way home.

I won a few awards for writing a poem. I hoped and prayed that my mom was going to be proud of me especially with the hundred dollar cash prize I'd won. It was the first time that I have ever won a cash prize for something that I wrote. See, I was the creative one; I always wrote poems and different things. It was my only outlet for emotions. Whenever I was hurting or in deep in thought, I would write.

I think I put my whole life down on paper because I wasn't good with expressing myself verbally. I don't know why I was excited to show my mom that I won this award because she never cared about anything I've done in school neither me or my brother. She would show some kind of compassion for my younger sisters but that was my mother. She loved them more because they had a different father than my brother and I, and he never put his hands on her. Maybe that's why she loved them more, but then again, she would whip them too, but never as bad as me or my brother.

When she did whip them, it was because their father didn't stay over with her. I believe that was her excuse for their beatings.

Anyway, I was on my way home to show off my accomplishments from school. When I walked through the door, I saw my mom sitting on the couch chuckling with this guy named Henry. He was a tall light skinned man with wavy hair a handsome face and a bright smile. But what stuck out to me was his uniform.

His uniform said that he was a part of the law. I thought that was a plus, because if he stayed around long enough he'd see what my mom really did to us and just maybe he would have her arrested for it and we would be free from this nightmare.

As I walked closer to them sitting on the couch, my mom asked if I was gonna stand there and stare or was I gonna speak. I couldn't really move because I was stunned by his authority. Man, did my soul cry out!

So my mom took the initiative and introduced me to him. As she said his name he stood up and held his hand out to shake mine.

It was like everything was moving in slow motion. I shook his hand and said that it was nice to meet him. My mother then told me to go to my room so that she and Henry could be alone. As I turned away, I had almost forgot about my prize. So I went back and told my mom that I won something that day. She acted surprised, as if she was happy that I won the award, I was confused, but I went with it.

He was happy as well, he complimented me and said that not only was I beautiful but I was smart as well. I showed my mom the certificates; she looked at them, smiled and said that she was proud of me. I told her that I got a cash prize for my poetry. She took the money and said that she was going to put it up so that when I wanted or needed something she would let me spend it. I was in the twilight zone, I may have been confused, but I took that moment for what it was and excused myself.

My brother was in our room playing with his toys and I had asked him about Henry. He told me that our mother said for him to be nice and keep quiet in the room until he left.

I also told my brother about the award that I won. He made fun of me as he always did and calling me a bookworm but that was part of the fun we shared between the two of us.

A while later, my mom's friend had left, that's when she called me into the living room and began talking to me about him. She actually accused me of flirting with him because when he complimented me I smiled at him but it wasn't him I was smiling at. It was the compliment he gave me and him not knowing me but being proud of me is what made me smile.

I'm sure she thought he wanted me and I knew that no man could ever want me with my ugly black ass. Once again, my mother changed like the weather. She was an angel as long as he was here but as soon as he left, she became the devil's right hand man. She then accused me of showing off in front of him, and said that I paraded my awards around like I was better than her.

She took my certificates, tore them in half and threw them in my face. I stood motionless as she called me names, from dumb bitch to whore and believe me that's the nice way of putting it.

After telling me to get out of her face, I had the nerve to turn around and asked her about my money I won. She charged at me with rage, grabbed me by my collar and told me that I wasn't getting a dime from her. She said that the money belonged to her and if I wanted it, then come and take it. The screaming made my brother and sisters come out of our room to see what all the cursing and fighting was about.

They watched our mother stomp me to the floor. As she told me to stay away from Henry and when he came around I'd better keep my eyes to the floor and not even look at him the next time he came over.

She left me in the middle of the floor with a busted lip. As my brother and two sisters came to see about me, she yelled from the other room, telling them to leave me alone. "Let that bitch bleed!" she said.

My brother went and got me a cold towel and placed it on my lip. I whispered to him to go to his room before he got into trouble. He said that he didn't care, he wanted to stay with me but I wasn't going to let him get a beating, so I got up and went to our room with him.

A new door of disrespect opened for my mother. She showed me that no matter what I accomplished in school, she'd never be proud of me but then again I shouldn't be surprised. I mean, she never showed me any affection before, why would she start now?

So as time went on, her new boyfriend Henry visited quite often. He went from spending nights to spending weeks. Soon after that, he was living with us and just so that I could stay out their way, I buried myself in my room writing in my journal. I remember one day he was at work and my mom called me out of the room and told me that I was supposed to clean the kitchen. I was upset at the fact that I had very little help when it came to cleaning the house. I think she saw that expression I had on my face. That made her angry.

"You got a problem with that?" She asked.

I lowered me eyes to the floor. "No." But as always, it registered differently in her mind.

When I said no, she took it as though I said yes. Then the gloves came off. She took everything out of the kitchen cabinets and told me to wipe them down, including the canned goods. Everything had to be wiped down and put back neat and perfect.

She came in periodically to make sure that I was doing things to her liking. The next time my mom came in the kitchen she looked at the stove and saw that it had not been cleaned yet.

"Bitch! What's taking you so long to clean this stove?"

She said that I needed some fire under my ass so that I could move faster. Coming from my mother that meant literally. She turned the stove on, snatched me by my arm and proceeded to put my hand on the burner. I pulled away from her and cradled my hand as though she did burn me. It was the thought of her really burning my hand that gave me that scare.

She walked out the kitchen and said that the kitchen better be cleaned by the time she got done using the bathroom. She said by the time she wiped her ass, I'd better be mopping my way out the kitchen and turning off the light. Lord knows, I knew she wasn't playing. So I made it my business to have everything done spotless, just the way she wanted it.

Though it was late when I got done. I still managed to do my homework and get a few hours of sleep.

The months dragged on, I took what my mother said to heart. I stayed out of hers and Henry's way. When I got out of school, I would head straight to my room. I was almost like a ghost. I avoided them for as long as I could.

Henry came home one day while my mom was out and my brother and sisters were playing in the living room. When he came in, he looked around for my mother, but she wasn't home so I ordered my brother and sisters to go to their rooms. As I cleaned the living area up, he asked when my mom would be back. I told him that I didn't know.

He sat on the couch, he began to compliment me.

"You're pretty. Those big eyes, that dark toned skin, Gonna be a beauty some day. For sure."

"Thank you," I mumbled as I kept my head down, facing the floor. He told me to come to him.

He asked, "Why do you always look so sad? You are too pretty to look sad."

As I walked closer to him, in my mind, I kind of thought that he cared. His asking me about my well-being might mean that he actually gave a damn.

No one has ever asked me how I felt or if I was okay. So it was strange when he then told me to sit on his lap and tell him what the problem was. As bad as I wanted to just spill my heart out I couldn't, because again that feeling that my mother was on her way in was all over me.

Henry went on to say that I could talk to him about anything.

"I'm your friend," he told me. "You know I wouldn't do anything to hurt you, right?" I felt secure with him, he seemed to be a stand-up guy and I did feel safe for a minute, but there was no way that I could be sitting on his lap when my mom came in so I got up and hustled to my room.

I didn't know what to feel about him; all I knew was that he made me feel like he cared. Which was something that I hadn't felt in a long time. Maybe in forever. My own father might have been a lot of things, but he never made us feel safe. So whatever attention I was getting at the moment was okay with me.

Later that night, I heard a squeaking sound outside my bedroom door. I thought it was my brother Donte, so I turned my head to see if it was him leaving. But he was still sleeping, so the shadow under the door was someone else.

I heard the sound of Henry's voice calling out to me in a whisper. What he wanted, I didn't know and I couldn't care because my mother was home. I just hoped and prayed she didn't catch him at my bedroom door. So I laid there, still and quiet, praying that he'd leave and just let me be.

The next morning, I don't think I got out for school so fast before in my life. I didn't want be in the same room with him and my mom. I feared he was going to say something to me that would make my mom upset and I'd never hear the end of it. So to avoid that situation, I got dressed for school in record time and shot out the front door.

CHAPTER 6

While my friends and I waited outside the school for classes to begin, we talked of ditching and going back to our friend's house and spend the school day there. We all agreed and slithered off the playground.

As soon as we got there, we turned the TV on and pigged out on some junk food we got from the store. We laughed as we talked about the shows we watched. I'd bury ourselves in the fairytale lifestyles that kids lived on TV. This was one time we weren't segregated, what I was going through was the same things they were going through, because through the eyes of television we all had the same problems.

Just for a moment, I pretended that the lives of *Leave it to Beaver* were us. I wanted that loving and caring mother that Beaver had and I'd wished that I was one the orphans that Mr. Drummond adopted on *Different Strokes*.

But this was my reality, and I promised myself that I would never be in the same predicament that my parents were in and vowed to not beat my kids like my mom did me.

We always planned our lives for when we got older because when we got our kids, we didn't want to take them through the same things that we were going through. Talks of our future took all day. As it got closer to the time for us to be making our way home, we wrapped up our garbage and began walking home just as if we were coming from school. As I approached my house, laughter filled the apartment. I opened the door and there I was my mother, Henry and my two sisters playing. My mom sat at the kitchen table as Henry played with Desire and Deonna. They spoke to me as I made my way to my room. My brother was chillin as usual.

It had been at least an hour after I came home when I heard a knock at the front door while I was doing my homework. I went to go see who it was and to my surprise, it was my friend and her mom. My mother asked who it was from in the kitchen; I said it was someone for her.

As I looked at my friend, she hung her head in shame because she knew that we vowed not to tell that we ditched school. So anyway, my mom asked my friend's mother how she was doing.

She replied "Mad as hell, because your daughter and my daughter decided to ditch school today".

I could have shit bricks. Mind you that my mom was in the kitchen cutting potatoes to make French fries and she was holding a big butcher's knife in her hand. So you know I feared for my life.

Soon after my friend's mother told her about me and my friend ditching school, they began to laugh and talk about another subject while I escaped to my room.

It was one of those times when I wished that I could just blink my eyes and be somewhere else. I got sick to my stomach, thinking of the consequences that I was going to suffer once they left.

I wanted my mother and my friend's mom to just continue laughing and talking so that she would forget what the visit was about. They had to have stayed an hour or so. My so called friend sat in one spot the hold time looking nervous as ever. She didn't even utter one word. I tried to finish up my homework before they left, so I wouldn't be up all night getting it done.

When my mother came out of the kitchen, standing there with one hand on her hip and the other one holding the knife, all I could see was me pleading for my life.

The next thing I remember was my mother calling me out of my room.

"Bring your ass here," she commanded, standing in the kitchen door with her two best friends: anger and hate.

These are the two she called when she wanted to have a party on my ass. Trust me, when they got together it was no laughing matter. She began to question me about where I had been and where did I go when I didn't go to school. I didn't get the chance to answer because before I knew it she was on my ass.

She pulled my hair and slapped me around.

"You think I got time to play around with your dumb ass?" she said as she shoved me to the floor.

She yelled that she had other kids to worry about other than me. She made it like I was causing all the trouble in the house.

When I got to my feet, she grabbed my neck with one hand while she punched me with her other hand. I was every dumb bitch and stupid ass in the book. She was no stranger to introducing her feet to my body either, they were well acquainted. My mother stomped me to floor followed by kicks to my back. She said since I wanted to be out of school, she was going to make sure that I was out by whipping my ass so bad that I wasn't going to be able to go.

I was still was taking my ass to school, no matter what, black eye and all. I'm saying to myself, *this bitch is crazy*, she don't care about how she's marking up my body for the public to see. Damn! Will she stop already?

That wasn't the first nor the last time I ditched school. I just tried to be more careful when I did it so that my mother wouldn't find out. It was my way of getting away from all the abuse I suffered in my home.

I felt so alone in this world; there was no one to talk to. So I used to sit in my room and talk to myself. Asking myself why me? Anybody that watched me in my room would say that I was talking to God but I couldn't say that because I was never taught about God. So if talking and asking why questions aloud was talking to God, then I guess that's what I was doing.

My mom and Henry had been together for quite some time now, she was taking a liking to him and I didn't see him leaving any time soon.

Which was another reason why I began to run away from home a lot. One day I ditched school again, well, I had in-school suspension so I felt there was no need to go, so I went over to my boyfriend's house. My boyfriend was all I had at the time his name was Mike and he was the finest man in the world to me at the time. He was about five eleven and he was light complected. He was also very intelligent; that alone turned me on about him. He didn't know much about my issues at home because I was pretty embarrassed about my situation because his family was well together, well from what I saw. He was my safe haven at the time and he made me feel important and loved. While I was there, the school notified my mother that I was suspended and I didn't show up after school. Later, when I got home, it was the start of World War III.

Soon as I came through the door she was like. "Oh, so yo dumb ass wanna cut school again huh and sit up in some boy's house?"

I was saying to myself, how in the hell do she know?

"And don't think I don't know about that boy you was with, either." That day she beat me at a minimum. That's because she wanted Henry to beat me as well.

She told him what happened and she wanted him to take me up stairs to the attic to whip me. When Henry took me up there, he gave me this speech about how I wanted to be a grown woman and that he was going to show me how grown women get treated. This was one of those moments that I wished for a loving mother to be in my life. Then he told me to take off my clothes.

He stood there and studied my body for a minute. He then touched my breast, asking me how it felt. I don't know what my mother thought was going to take place up in the attic, but it damn sure wasn't just whipping my ass.

He was touching me the way he should be touching my mother. I have never been so scared. It was so sickening to me to have someone to touch you without your permission or for someone to violate your privacy like this.

My mother wouldn't have believed me if I told her what Henry was doing, because I always knew she loved him more than me.

After he got his fill of my body, he whipped me. And told me to take my grown ass downstairs. I wish that I can say this was the last time he touched me, but it wasn't. I finally got so fed up with my mother beating me and Henry molesting me that I ran away. I stayed gone for about three days.

When I returned, Henry hugged me, telling me that I didn't have to run away because they loved me so much and they didn't want me to leave or run away like that again.

What a crock of shit, I said to myself. After he said what he had to say he then squeezed my butt; it was more like a grope.

But this was the result of being in a situation where as you feel like your back is up against the wall. Outside of my writing and going over to my friend's house, I had no other ways of getting away from the pain that was inflicted on me at home. I had a mother that hated me, a step-father that molested me, two younger sisters that envied me and a brother that I feared wouldn't ever know how to be a loving parent because all he been around is a mother that showed no love toward him.

I just didn't feel like we were going to have promising futures because my mother never encouraged us to do our best in school or aim for what we wanted in life.

It's like she had to endure us because we were her kids and she was just giving us room and board until we reached the age to be on our own. If you ask me, we all were being punished. She was stuck with raising us and we were stuck with her abusing us.

There were days that I went without food and there were days when I cleaned the whole house and was not rewarded for it. I know kids are supposed to do chores, but damn, I was the only kid in the house that had to do them, seems like.

One day after school, my mother was standing waiting for me. She informed me I had a lot of work to do. What she meant was, I had countless hours of work. I mean, she had me to wash our clothes in the bathtub; I scrubbed the floors on my hands and knees. I took the pictures off the walls and shelves and dusted. I was cleaning from the time I got home until it was time to go to bed. I missed dinner and everything, but then again, no I didn't, because she cooked dinner and had my brother and sisters sit at the table and eat.

But as for me, I was still cleaning and scrubbing clothes. By the time I got done, it was time for bed. I went to tell my mom that I was done cleaning she told me that the kids were done with their dinner; I thought she was going to tell me to go and fix my plate.

But she told me to go wash the dishes and go to bed. I told her that I didn't eat.

She said, "What the hell has that got to do with me? If your ass had got done with your chores, you would have been able to sit down with everybody else and eat!"

I turned away like a homeless person turned away from a shelter that was over crowed. As I cleaned the kitchen I glanced at the food they threw away, even the food in the garbage looked good to me. That night I went to bed hungry. That was the worst though. The worst was knowing this time, she didn't just lose her temper and start beating on me. She'd planned this one in advance.

CHAPTER 7

Things got worse each and every day. There were countless times I got beatings. If anyone was to ask me what my most vivid memories as a child were, I'd say it was the beatings because I got a whole lot of those and they were all something to remember. They only got worse as I got older, because as I grew into a teenager, she felt increasingly threatened by the young woman I was becoming. Maybe she was even jealous.

I can't talk about the gifts I got as child for Christmas or anything like that. My sisters were the ones that got everything.

My mom had a longtime friend that cared for me, named Delores. She knew the way that my mom was treating me so she became my godmother. She bought me clothes, gave me candy and made sure I didn't want for anything. It was like she was heaven sent.

She knew my every need and she actually showed me love, I mean some genuine love. She didn't want anything from me; all she wanted was for me to be happy and treated fair. That burned my mother up; she didn't like the fact that I was getting so much attention and my sisters weren't.

It was almost like I was Cinderella and they were my evil step sisters. Any and everything I got nice or rewarded with came from my godmother. Then my mother would take it and tell me I didn't deserve shit. But she would always wait until Delores left before she would take the things from me and give them to my sisters. It's like to her, I wasn't allowed to be happy; only my stepsisters deserved to be happy and enjoy the finer things in life.

My godmother had been in my life for a long time but I was never able to tell her how my mother took the stuff she had given me. Because my mom would threaten me. She told me that if I opened my mouth and told my Delores what happened she was going to whip my ass. I knew what that was like. I was a silent mutha fucker, I kept her dirty little secrets.

Even the kids in our neighborhood knew how mean my mother was. When she'd go to work they used to look out for her so I could come outside and play for about ten or fifteen minutes at a time. Just so that I could come and play with them. I mean, the sun would be shining and the temperature was just right and I had to stay in the house. Sometimes I'd have to stay in while my sisters got to go out and play. It was my job to make sure that nothing happened to them.

I had to watch them from the porch and you guessed right. I was told not to step one foot away from it, either. On one occasion, my sisters wanted to play with some girls that stayed further up the street, but that would have been too far for me to see, so I told them no. They didn't listen, of course. So they took off running and naturally I came off the porch to chase them. When I did that, they stopped running. My sister Deonna turned and told me that she was going to tell our mother that I left the porch.

Seeing the expression on their faces, I know they did it on purpose. They were upset because I told them that they couldn't go to their friend's house. And they knew that my mom was going to believe them over me.

See, this is how they got their way with me. They'd always threaten me with my mother. They played that, *'she loved them more than me'* game. They played it to the hilt.

Deonna and Desire knew that's how my mom felt so

every time they wanted to see me get into trouble they would tell my mom that I hit them or I didn't feed them while she was at work. Anything to get my ass whipped. Sometimes I swear, every time I got a whooping they were somewhere around the corner, laughing.

There was a set time when I had to have them back in the house. I had to have them back in the house by 6:00pm. But since they pulled that stunt I made them come in early, and I waited until about 6:30pm to feed them.

I was told to make them sandwiches because my mother was on her way home and she was going to start dinner. So I went through the trouble of fixing all of us sandwiches and them two heifers didn't even eat. I begged them to eat, but they wanted to be able to tell my mother that I didn't feed them. So I called my brother to the kitchen table and we ate. At about 7:00 pm my mom walked through the door.

She saw me and my brother Donte sitting at the table, eating. She asked where Deonna and Desire were. I told her they were in our room. She then asked if they had eaten and I said no. So she called them to her and she asked why they weren't eating with us. These two so-in-so's told my mother that I said I wasn't going to feed them. Now mind you, she asked them why I said that I wasn't going to feed them and they couldn't even come up with a reason.

Every time I opened my mouth to defend myself she told me to shut the fuck up. They then told her that I left off the porch. Now all of this information is registering to my mother that I'm being grown and trying to run her house.

She slapped me so hard I literally saw lighting and fell out the kitchen chair. She then said if Deonna and Desire are not eating then ain't a mutha fucka in this house eating.

Everybody went to bed hungry. All but my brother and I at least went to bed on a half full stomach.

After telling us to go to bed, my mom waited until about two o'clock in the morning before she came into our room and woke me up by beating me with a belt. She beat me all the way to the kitchen. With sleep in my eyes I tried to focus on what she was telling me to clean. She had a hand full of my skin as she grabbed me in the back of my neck. She said that I took my dumb ass to bed leaving the kitchen nasty and full of dishes.

I reminded her that she's the one that made me go to bed before I could do it. She shoved me into the kitchen sink so hard, that it put a bruise on my stomach.

I wiped my eyes and tried to feel my way around to get the detergent to wash the dishes with. I must have been moving a little too slow because she began yelling at me telling me to hurry up.

She kept slapping me in my face and eye from behind making it hard for me to see. Between the tears from crying and the burning from her nails going into my eyes from her slapping me, it was hard for me to see.

I guess I still wasn't moving fast enough because she went and got an extension cord and began striking me across my back. She still wasn't satisfied because she made me get undressed. She wanted me to feel the lashes from the cord.

So now I'm standing at the kitchen sink naked, trying to wash the dishes and my mom wasn't making it easy. She kept ranting about the things my sisters said I'd done. The more I tried to plead my case, the more she beat. Now I'm seeing blood. The cuts from her hitting me with the extension cord were starting to blister up and bleed. But that didn't stop her from beating me. That night she beat so badly, I could hardly walk.

Once I finally got done, she sent me to my room. It hurt so bad to even lie down in my bed. The next morning, when my brother and sisters were getting ready for school, my brother was worried that I was going to let our mother catch me still in bed and not ready for school.

Usually I could tough it out after a beating and still get up with a smile, ready for school. But not this time, when I woke up the next day the eye she kept hitting me in was so swollen I couldn't hardly open it.

My sheets had blood on it from the cuts and blisters from the cord she whipped me with. My body was so stiff I just couldn't move. Once my mother saw that I wasn't among the others leaving out for school, she came in my room, ready to beat me again because I wasn't up and ready for school. But she saw the blood on my sheets, and she peeled them back slowly. That's when she saw the blisters from the whipping the night before. She then turned me over and saw my eye was so swollen that I couldn't even see out of it.

That day my mother acted a little bit like a caring mother, but this, too was part of her pattern. When she saw that she beat us too bad she would act as though she gave a damn. But now I know she was only doing it because she wanted me to keep quiet, and help her to hide my bruises, black eyes and busted lips. She told me that if I told anyone, no one was going to do anything but call some people to come and take me from our house and I'd end up lost in the system; I wouldn't be able to be found.

I guess this was her way of trying to scare us into not telling anyone. I thought anywhere was better than being here, but when she mentioned that I wouldn't see my little brother anymore, it always made me think twice. So that morning she helped me out of bed and walked me to the kitchen, and assisted me as I sat down at the table. Once I got situated, she got me some ice for my eye and began cooking me some breakfast. As I sat there watching my mom cook for me, I was ecstatic because it's very rare that she did things like this for me. But deep down I knew she wasn't sorry she just wanted me to hide my bruises.

She cooked me a nice breakfast and at the same time she comforted me with kind words. She said that when she got paid, she was going to buy me that doll that I always wanted. And with Christmas under a week away, I felt good because I was going to have something under the tree this year.

She cared for me the whole day and when it came time for my brother and sisters to come home she told them not to bother me, let me get some rest and she would be home later to cook for us.

I was out of school for about three days, long enough for the swelling to go down in my eye, and that's when I returned to school.

During lunch, a few teachers did notice the black eye, but they also had noticed on a few occasions but I would say that I ran into a door while playing with my brother.

I'm sure they thought that I was having a lot of accidents. As far as the bruises on my body, they couldn't see those because my mom would always dress me up in clothes that hid them. Just like when I went without dinner, I used to go to school and eat my friend's lunch. They thought I had a big appetite, but it was because the night before my mother sent me to bed without dinner. So by the time I got to school I was hungry.

By the time my mom's check came all that loving and caring attitude she'd showed me went out the window. By that time, my wounds had healed, there was still some soreness but it wasn't enough for my mom to buy me what she said was going to. And now that we were out for Christmas break, it was like a roller coaster ride, I was back down at the bottom of the barrel, and I was no longer my mother's first priority.

On Christmas day, we rushed to see what we got; this was supposed to be one of the happiest times in a child's life. But as for me it was like Halloween; it was scary because though I wanted something I knew I wasn't getting anything.

So I sat there with the rest of my siblings, waiting for my name to be called to get a gift. The more I saw my sisters get, the fewer presents I saw under the tree. I then knew there was nothing for me.

I got up and went to my room and just cried. I mean she didn't offer any explanation why I didn't get a present or nothing. It was like I was supposed to know that I wasn't going to get anything.

Later that day my godmother came over. After she talked with my mom for a while, she called me into the living room and asked me what I got for Christmas. I told her nothing, and she acted surprised, but then she wasn't, not really. She knew what type of person my mom was.

My Godmother even asked her why didn't I get anything. Mamma told her I did something in school that I had no business doing but Delores knew that wasn't true, so she comforted me for a while and told me not to cry; she wiped my tears away and told me she would be back later.

Once my godmother left, mom started yelling and cursing me out, saying that I was filling Delores' head with lies about her. So she told me to go to my room and if Delores came back with something for me, she made it clear that I wasn't getting a damn thing.

And she kept her word. When my godmother returned to our apartment about three hours later, she brought me a TV, clothes and some toys, like teddy bears and the baby dolls that I had always wanted. I was about eleven or twelve at the time and some would say I was too old for dolls but it was alright with me. My mom, sisters and brother gathered around as I opened my gifts. They all acted as though they were happy for me.

My sisters admired my TV and my brother was just glad to see that I was happy for once. I watched my mom from out the corner of my eye. She was giving me the nastiest look ever. I mean, it really bothered her that I had someone that actually gave a damn; that there was someone doing something for me. So after about two hours or so, my godmother told me to enjoy my gifts she then left.

I took my presents to our room and not to my surprise my two sisters followed me. They looked on as I plugged my TV up to watch it as I played with my teddy bears, and I had about four of them and three dolls.

My sisters came into our bedroom and asked questions like, why did she buy stuff for me and not them? Damn, as if they didn't have enough toys already. They wanted to watch my TV and I told them no because they were going to break it. They said that I thought that I was all that because somebody bought me something for Christmas. I denied their allegations and went on to play with my new toys. They still refused to leave the room. They stood in the doorway, asking to play with my toys. I reminded them that they had their own toys to play with but they insisted on playing with mine. After hearing them whine about my TV I got up and shut the door on them.

A few seconds later here come the big bad wolf. My mother slammed the door open, yelling about how I thought my TV was too good for someone to play with. I said no, but she still came into our room and took my TV and turned it away from me so that it faced Deonna and Desire's side of the room. She then threw the clothes that my godmother bought me into a garbage bag and to make sure that I didn't go back and get them, she poured bleach on them and made my brother take the bag out to the dumpster.

She then told me that I better not tell Delores what she had done. Words could not express the way I felt. My heart was broken into pieces. I buried my face into my pillow and cried.

Just under two weeks later, we were all in our room. Well I was watching my TV and my sisters were playing with their dolls while my brother lay in his bed watching TV with me. Suddenly, an argument broke out between them over a doll.

They started to tussle. I ordered them to stop, but they carried on. Deonna started crying because Desire hit her. So Deonna shoved her right into my TV and it hit the floor. I got really angry. I told them to stop or else I was telling our mother. They both sat on Desire's bed, crying as I picked my TV off the floor to check it. That TV never came back on. I yelled at them even more, and that's when my mother came in to see what all the yelling and crying was about.

Before I could get a word in, my sisters told my mother that they were hitting each other over their toys. My mom inquired about my TV and I told her that they broke it while fighting. My mother said nothing at all; she let them do any and everything to me, and she never got on them for breaking my TV. She was more upset with them for fighting each other.

When I asked my mom about my TV, her attitude was like, what about your TV?

"If you'd broken them up and come and gotten me, it wouldn't have gotten broke in the first place." As usual, she blamed me. As if the abuse she was giving me wasn't enough. I couldn't win for losing.

Everything I did was wrong. I mean, I couldn't talk, I couldn't play, I couldn't do nothing but cater to them and my mom. And if it wasn't right I'd get beat for it. And she wondered why, when I got my report card I always had check marks in exercising self-control and too much talking.

I couldn't talk at home, so by the time I got to school I had a lot to say.

It felt good being able to talk to someone, shit, it felt good talking period. I also used to get check marks in working well in groups meaning I didn't do good in that area. I had two sisters and a brother that I couldn't interact with unless I was feeding them while our mom worked night shift. I have friends I wasn't allowed to go out and play with. So when did I have the time to know what it was like to work in groups? And trust and believe I got my ass whipped for every check mark I got, too.

One day, my sisters were playing through the house and it was a mess, they were getting a bit loud so our mother told them that she was going to take them to the park to get all of that yelling and screaming out of their systems. I naturally got happy because we were getting the chance to get out of the house for a change. As we all got ready and stood at the door, she asked me where the hell did I think I was going? I looked confused as I reminded her that she told us to get ready to go to the park. She said that she was only taking my sisters.

I felt so disappointed because I wanted to go and have fun too. And the only reason she took my brother was because she didn't want nobody talking to me. I did ask why I couldn't go, she said because I had to clean up the house. Excuse me, but Deonna and Desire are the ones that messed the house up so I felt that they should have cleaned up. But she made it clear that I didn't deserve to go with them and my place was here, scrubbing the floors. When I insisted my sisters should and could help me clean up because, after all, they're the ones that made the mess, she punched me right in my mouth busting my lips.

She then told me not to get smart with her.

"Now stay your ass here and clean this mutha fuckin' house up like I said. And it better be done by the time we get back".

As I stood there, trying to keep from crying, I saw my sisters making faces at me, teasing me about not being able to go. But they it did so that our mother couldn't see or hear them.

She then ushered them out the door. I turned and looked at the apartment, toys were everywhere. The kitchen had dirty dishes on the table and in the sink. My sisters threw their clothes all over the floor in our room. When my mom say clean the house, she meant the whole house. Everybody's room, the bathroom, kitchen, wherever. If it was part of the apartment, it had to be cleaned.

I collected all the toys from around the house and put them where they belonged. I then cleaned the bathroom; I got down on my knees and scrubbed the toilet, tub and floor.

Soon after I made my way to the kitchen, raking the old uneaten food off the plates, I then made some dishwater and began to wash them. I scrubbed the cabinets, stove and the floor. Then there was the living room, the toys were already put away so I dusted, swept and then I did the floor. It took me the whole day to get done with everything.

I went to my room, laid in my bed and began writing in my journal. It was starting to get late. They left for the park at about twelve in the afternoon. It was now 7:30pm and I was getting hungry. I paced back and forth, peeking out of the window to see if I saw them coming, I didn't want to take it upon myself to go get food out of the refrigerator, because that would make my mom beat me, so I tried waiting for them to get back.

I don't know where the time went, but I fell asleep in my room, that's when I heard them coming in. They laughed and talked about the fun they had while they were at the park. I walked to the living room to tell my mom that I was hungry. Everybody just took their shoes off, leaving them in the middle of the floor and threw their coats on the couch. Nobody took the time to see that I cleaned the house from top to bottom, nor did my mom recognize the work I put in. She just ordered everybody to go to bed.

I mentioned to her that I was hungry; she said that it was too late to be fixing something to eat. See, they ate while they were out, because they met up with Henry and he'd treated everybody to food. He wanted to bring me something back because he saw that I was missing, but my mom told him not to bring me anything. I didn't care anyway because he was a creep in my book. I would rather starve than take anything from him.

Sometimes I think that I was cursed, maybe I didn't live my past life right and now God was punishing me. I mean I've been stuck in this damn house all day, slaving my ass off with nothing to eat afterward. And they come home full and shit, and she tells me to go to bed. This can't be nothing but a fucking nightmare. She treated me like I was their live in slave instead of her child and I couldn't take no more.

Later that night, I was so hungry that my stomach was hurting. I got up and listened to make sure everyone was sleeping before I went into the kitchen to nab me something to eat. This was one ass whipping I was willing to take because I was hungry, I would have taken an ass whooping from anybody.

When the coast was clear, I tiptoed to the kitchen and grabbed me a hand full of Oreo cookies and ran straight to my room. I ate them cookies so fast I don't even remember chewing. I had to get something that was quick and didn't require a lot of effort getting.

The next morning while making my bed I noticed crumbs from the cookies. I hurried to brush my bed off so that my mom wouldn't find out that I had been eating cookies. As I was bent over brushing my bed off I turned and there I saw Henry, watching me like a cat watching its prey.

As he looked at me, he licked his lips like he just wanted to eat me or something. Urgently, I pulled my gown down over my butt and hung my head in shame. I was too busy worrying about him telling that I ate in my room.

But Henry was too busy watching me to notice what I was trying to hide. Before he could walk off, he winked at me, followed by blowing me a kiss telling me that he will see me later. And I knew what that meant; he was waiting on the perfect time to molest me again. I was already fed up with that, too. I was so ready to just run away and never come back.

Our first day back to school after the Christmas break, my mom called me to the kitchen so that she could straighten my hair for school. She would put like a pound of hair grease in my head and then put the hot comb to it. She'd burn the hell out of me three or four times, and get mad when I flinched from the pain. My mother hit me with the handle of the comb and brush just because I moved. Like I'm supposed to stay put while she burned the hell out me with the hot comb. After about four burns to my neck and forehead she then sat me down on the floor between her legs to braid my hair. As she turned me to her, what I saw made me sick to my stomach.

She had on some dirty panties and they weren't really pleasing to the eyes or nose. She took so long getting me ready I had missed breakfast already and I didn't get nothing for dinner the night before. So I had to rush to school just so I could make it to eat breakfast. It's a good thing they served breakfast at school or otherwise I'd pass out due to hunger before lunch time. When I caught up with my friends in the lunchroom, I saw they were all sitting there talking instead of eating their cereal, so I asked them if I could have it, I made it look like I just loved cereal and what I had wasn't enough. I didn't want them to know that I really went to bed hungry last night.

It wasn't the first time I went to school not hungry, but starving. There were many times my mother sent me to bed hungry and there were times when I had to do house work and watch the other kids eat. They went to bed with their stomachs full of food while I went to bed with my stomach full of hunger. And it was always some lame ass excuse as to why I had to go without dinner. And there also were times I went to school dressed like a nun because she was hiding the bruises I had all over my body from her beating me.

The teachers would sometimes ask questions but I'd tell lies to cover my mom's ass. So she wouldn't get into trouble or, as my mom would say, get us lost in the system. I'm sure that a lot kids get bullied by their mom or someone else, so that they won't tell anybody about the horror that's going on in their homes.

I had gotten to the point where I was sneaking out of the house while everybody was sleeping. I'd wait for my mom to go to sleep and I'd leave the door unlocked so that I could get in once I got back.

One night I went out and met up with some friends of mine. We would go to the arcade and just hang out. Laughter filled the air as we joked around and chased one another. We were young kids hanging in the streets at a very young age, but what saved us half the time was our friend Kira, because she was the tallest out of all of us and like me, she had a body like a grown woman. So not too many people asked us questions about being out past our bedtime.

Sometimes, when I was out all by myself, I'd just go to the park where all the other bigger kids hung out. I never went places that were dangerous. I was just glad to go somewhere that I can feel free of abuse.

Being with my godmother was one other time I felt free because one summer my God sister took me to Great America, the biggest amusement park there is. And boy, did I have fun, it was me and her and her best friend only, neither my brother nor my sisters went. And trust me, my mother tried to intervene. This was something else I was seeing about my mother, she did everything in her power to keep me from being happy. I was starting to think that she lived to make my life miserable. Nothing she did to me made me feel that she gave damn about me.

And I would think that if someone was willing to take any financial burdens or take a kid or two off her hands that she would be happy.

Only our misery made my mom happy, the cries of our wanting souls to feel like a normal family. The hunger we had of just wanting her to care, made her hateful love towards us smile with glee as she indulged her bitterness into our pure hearts of innocence. I don't know about my siblings, but I always fantasized about having a different mother. While other kids were at home probably playing with the toys that they've always wanted, I was at home having fantasies about having the things they had and things that I could call my own.

Nothing belonged to me, not even the air I breathed. Everything that I was blessed with or given was taken from me. Not by the strangers in the streets, but from the people who claimed to be put into my life to love me.

I was young and corrupted, I was becoming damaged goods before I could be of age to make my own mistakes and corrupt my own damn self.

Living each day in my house was like being in a prison and I felt like I was sentenced to life.

My mom did a good job at running people away that she thought meant us some good. I don't know what she thought that she was going to accomplish by doing everything she could to make sure me and my brother didn't have the things we needed or wanted. At first, I was thinking that it was because of who our father was and what he did to her, but now I'm having a change of heart.

But what would be the excuse, now that he's gone? Our father left a long time ago and she still beat us.

It was towards the end of the school year. We all couldn't wait for the summer to come because that's when we had the chance to get out and have some fun with our friends.

My fun was limited because my mom always found reasons for me and my brother to be stuck in the house doing housework. She would always have him cleaning out the closets and taking out the garbage while I was scrubbing walls and floors.

But one day after school my brother and I were cleaning the house when the phone rang. From the sound of the conversation it was from our school. See, we went to a charter school and they had very low tolerance for misbehaved kids.

My brother's teacher called to tell my mom that he was being disruptive in class. At first, I thought the call was for me so I hurried up and finished my chores and ran to our room and did what they called laid low.

How I found out that the call was for my brother was when I heard my mother cursing him out about being the class clown. She then escorted Dante into our bedroom.

She told him to get undressed while she wrapped the cord around her hand as she prepared to whoop my brother. Before she could start whipping him, he started crying. He was starting to take too long of a time getting undressed, so my mom beat him out of his clothes.

She didn't like the fact that he was moving around to avoid getting hit. It was becoming to be too much work so she tied him to the post of our bunk beds to keep him in one place. She beat my brother Donte for a long time, to the point where as his welts were starting to bleed.

She kept telling him to shut up as if she was trying to keep him quiet so that the neighbors wouldn't hear his screams for mercy. I felt so bad for him because he was so little and he was at the age where he's expected to be a little disruptive. But like I said, she treated us like we were supposed to know things already. She preached and then she beat, she preached and then she beat, that was her routine.

I turned my head to the wall because I didn't want to see how bad she was beating him. I even tried leaving the room, but she told me to sit my ass back down, as if she wanted me to watch. I think it was because she knew how bad it bothered me to see her beat him the way she did.

I watched my mother beat my little brother until his back was covered in blood. She didn't care; she just kept beating him with this cord used for hanging wet clothes out to dry. And if she was doing this to him, I can't imagine what she would do to me if I tried to step in and help.

After she got done whipping Dante, she went to untie him from the post of our bunk beds, he fell to the floor shaking; it seemed almost like he was having a seizure, I was scared as hell. I screamed for my mother and she came in our room and looked at him and said that there was nothing wrong with him. Then she just walked away.

I couldn't do nothing but hold him, without trying to irritate the deep cuts on his back. Donte finally settled down. His body was still shivering from the aftershocks of my mother's beating. She didn't even come back to see if he was okay after that and I was left again to pamper his wounds.

This was another time when I wished that we had someplace else to go like our sisters did. Their father came by almost every weekend and took them to his house or somewhere they could let their hair down and be kids and have fun. We were always left behind to do nothing.

I went into the bathroom, got a warm towel and nursed my brother's wounds. His back was covered in bruises, outside of the welts that covered his back. I didn't sleep in my bed that night; I slept with him so he could feel safe. I did this every time my mom beat him, because he'd always fear that my mom would come back and whoop him some more.

There were a few times when he was afraid to go to sleep at night because of the beatings he got. At times he'd wake up crying and screaming and I would have to climb out of my bunk to comfort him.

I spent many nights comforting Donte, like a big sister protecting him from the boogie man. That's how he saw my mother, like some type of a hideous monster that was out to destroy us. All my brother and I had was each other. We looked out and protected one another. That's why we took each other's whippings, it was like we had a bond with one another and that's how we made it through our childhood years. It was a treat to see to my little sisters get into trouble or get a whipping, sad to say, but true. But they were never as bad as mine or my brother's.

She was always easy on them, even when they got into trouble at school. My mom would say that she's taking their toys away, but ended up giving them right back. It was almost like they could do no wrong. When one of them was sick she waited on them hand and foot. She took Deonna and Desire back and forth to the doctor making sure that they had the proper medicines to get better.

When it came to me and my brother, we suffered; we'd go days without care. My mother acted as though it was a punishment to her to give us medicine or take us to go get physicals. Any and everything about us was agony to her.

I gave up on wanting to know how it feels to be loved and wanted by my mother, the one that gave birth to me. Because if I couldn't get it from her then I thought that maybe I didn't deserve to know what love was and how it could feel.

So what becomes of a child that wasn't motherless physically but motherless mentally and emotionally? To me, that's where it counted. Just because you have a baby doesn't makes you a mother. It's the love, caring and attention, with a long list of other nurturing expressions that makes a loving mother.

I don't know what the hell gave birth to me. Sometimes I tell myself the devil himself had something to do with this.

Any mother that worked so hard to see her children hurt and not be happy can't possibly be a mother from this earth. The tension in my house was becoming too much to handle. That's what drove me to sneak out of the house like I was doing; fleeing to the nearby parks and hanging with kids older than me.

I even had a crush on one of boys that hung out there with us. That was another reason why I made it my business to be there. Just to laugh and enjoy the freedom of being away from the house.

No one knew that I was leaving. I'd just leave the door unlocked so I could get back in when I returned. But on this particular night, things didn't go according to my plan.

It was a beautiful cool night and I was heading to the park where everybody hung out. The night was young with a dusk of daylight still partially filling the sky. The stars was about to make their debut and it was just the perfect night to see my special friend; I thought that nothing could spoil this magical night for me.

As I made my way to the park I looked up at the sky periodically, rehearsing what I was going to say to my friend Devin once I got there. I even made sure that I looked good enough to catch his eye so that he could give me the attention I wanted from him. He was a nice and sweet boy. He was always respectful, kind of quiet and he'd always speak to me with a wink. Yeah, I was young, but I knew that this was the first time that someone looked at me and it felt comfortable besides my first so called boyfried.

I mean, if he felt the same way, he sure had a respectful way of showing it and that was enough for me. At least he wasn't twenty or thirty years older than me, trying to get me to do unwilling things with him. As I got to the park, everybody was there, as usual, and like always, who did I see giving me the eye? It was Devin, standing among his friends, laughing and talking. As I sat with the girls, thinking about what I was going to say when I go over to talk to him something stopped me in my tracks. Devin was on his way over to me. My heart pounded as he walked closer to us, my words lost in my anticipation of what was the reason for his coming over.

After Devin said his hellos to all the girls, he asked me if I wanted to take a walk. I stumbled over my words, but said yes. We walked about three feet or so away from everyone else. He asked about me, my likes and dislikes. I felt so good talking to him because he didn't have a motive for asking me these questions other than wanting to get to know me.

And that was alright with me. I told Devin that I loved to write poetry. There wasn't much to tell because a lot of times I didn't have the freedom to explore a lot of different things. So I talked a long time about my writing and what I hoped to do with it when I got older. He told me that he loved playing basketball and he wanted to pursue it professionally.

It was like the perfect night. Though it was getting older. I didn't care because I was lost in Devin's charm as a young man. I was twelve going on thirteen and he was fifteen and to me, we made the perfect match.

He offered me some of his candy and I accepted as if he bought it especially for me. Man! We must have laughed until we were in tears. We then held hands and headed over to the swings.

I got on; Devin pushed me for a while, then got on the swing next me. We talked more about school and each other.

We saw that everybody was starting to leave, but we were so lost in each other that time had gotten away from us. As we walked back over to the group, everyone was leaving; Devin asked his friend what time was it. It was well after eleven o'clock.

He offered to walk me home and of course I agreed. Devin walked me about a block away from my house, then turned and walked home himself. But not before an innocent kiss on the cheek to seal the night. I watched him walk a few feet away before I went on and made my way home.

I approached my building and went into the hallway; I quietly turned the door knob. My heart stopped. I went to try and enter my apartment and the door was locked. Someone, probably my mother, had woken up and locked me out.

More than likely, it would have been the end of my young life if my mother had come to the door and seen me standing outside trying to get in. So I leaned up against the wall with disappointment, wondering what I was going to do. It was already near midnight. I had left the house without anyone knowing and the locked door was the least of my worries.

I thought that maybe I could knock on the door loud enough for my brother to hear, but quiet enough so that my mom wouldn't be awakened by my brother making the necessary effort to let me in.

I was in for the one of the worst whippings of my life if I went through with that plan. I sat on the floor in the hallway of my building in front of my apartment door, running all kinds of ways to get into the house without my mom finding out. But every plan that I came up with would have resulted in waking her. And I just couldn't go through a beating right now, it would've spoiled my perfect night with Devin. So eventually, I got up and left.

I had no clue where I was going or what I was going to do. But anything would have been better than getting beaten to a pulp by my mother that night. I went back to the park, which was completely deserted, even though teenagers had filled it less than an hour before.

I sat on the same swing that I sat on when I was there with Devin. Where in the hell was I going? After I got tired of sitting there I walked the streets some more. I was getting tired but I refused to go home.

Just as I was walking down a street blocks from my house I ran into a friend. He spoke to me, followed by questioning why I was out that late. I told him what happened and what landed me on the street that time of night. So I asked him if I could stay with him for the night. He agreed and there we were, walking up the street to his house.

AFTERWORD

This is just the first of many chapters in my life and I am sharing them with you. I mean how much more can a child take?

Let the journey begin!

BIOGRAPHY

Danette Mckinley has been a fighter all of her life. Born July 30th 1974 in Chicago, IL, she has faced and overcome many adversities, including coming from a broken family and entering the judicial system at a very young age.

Danette currently has seven children, including one that's deceased. She had her first child at the age of fourteen after suffering multiple forms of abuse. Danette has dedicated her life to changing the lives and views of the youth of today. She has performed multiple services and given countless donations to the Austin Township Community and has worked for other communities and organizations to help establish a healthier living environment for today's urban youth.

Through her love and passion for children and impoverished teens, in 2007, she founded Young Creative Minds (YCM) youth organization. Which has etched quite a reputation for itself?

She created and facilitated the famous Westside spelling bee within the Austin community. This event catered to the Chicago public school district to promote literacy, awareness and good sportsmanship among peers, as well as scholastic acceleration.

YCM landscaping service takes teenagers that were either on probation or paroled and gives them option to complete their community service through this program. They also have an opportunity to become employed for their services.

The community salute concert series is yet another innovative way to give back to her community. She orchestrated a free concert for under privileged children whom couldn't afford tickets to see their favorite artists.

Just to name a few of her many attributes Danette uses her past pains as her strength in order to pave a road for children and young adults that has or are currently traveling a path that she once traveled.

From speaking of past pains from abusive and non-cohesive relationships to dealing one on one with Chicago underground drug cartels, she continues to inspire young women and young men to be more than what the system has labeled them, which is another statistic.

Danette has received multiple accolades from city aldermen and even former Mayor Richard H. Daley. As long as she continues to be a pillar of the urban community and a champion for youth, she is sure to receive much more in the future.

1 Peter 4:8

And above all things be earnest in your love among yourselves, for Love covers a multitude of sin...

Available now part 2…

Betrayal of the Streets

By

Danette King